Everything You Need to Know About

BEING A VEGETARIAN

More people are choosing a vegetarian diet every day.

· THE NEED TO KNOW LIBRARY ·

Everything You Need to Know About

BEING A VEGETARIAN

Kim Serafin

THE ROSEN PUBLISHING GROUP, INC.
NEW YORK

To my parents, who have always supported me in every life decision,
including my choice to become a vegetarian.

Published in 1999 by The Rosen Publishing Group, Inc.
29 East 21st Street, New York, NY 10010

First Edition

Library of Congress Cataloging-in-Publication Data

Serafin, Kim.
    Everything you need to know about being a vegetarian / Kim Serafin.— 1st ed.
      p. cm. — (The need to know library)
    Includes bibliographical references and index.
    Summary: Discusses the different motivations and special nutritional needs of vegetarians, the different kinds of vegetarianism, and ways to change to a vegetarian diet.
    ISBN 0-8239-2951-5 (lib. bdg.)
    1. Vegetarianism—Juvenille literature. [1. Vegetarianism.] I. Title. II. Series.
  TX329.S39 1999
  613.2'62 — dc21
                                          99-13244
                                            CIP

Manufactured in the United States of America

Contents

Introduction   6

1. What and Who Are Vegetarians?   11

2. Why Be a Vegetarian?   16

3. Talking to Your Family and Friends   24

4. How to Get Started   29

5. Nutrition and Staying Healthy   39

6. Special Occasions   46

7. Sample Recipes and Meal Ideas   52

Glossary   57

For Further Reading   59

Where to Go for Help   60

Index   63

Introduction

*V*egetarian. You've heard the word before. You have read that your favorite rock star keeps a vegetarian diet. You've seen it at the bottom of a menu at a restaurant: We offer several vegetarian entrees. Maybe you've ordered the vegetarian pasta once or twice.

Or maybe you think that a vegetarian is someone who eats only vegetables. Worse, you have heard the word associated only with hippies or out-of-control activists. You think that to be a vegetarian, you would have to leave your family, sell your worldly possessions, and move to a commune. You might have to carry around a sign with a big peace symbol and vow to rid the earth of every McDonald's restaurant.

But wait. Before you start shopping for tie-dyed T-shirts and drafting legislation to outlaw hamburgers, there are a few things that you should know:

Vegetarianism is a common dietary and lifestyle choice. In fact, over 15 million North Americans consider themselves vegetarians. Since you've picked up this book, you might have already met a few vegetarians and have become curious. Maybe a teacher or coach has mentioned something about being a vegetarian. Perhaps one of your friends has been eating things like tofu and tempeh instead of ham and cheese, and you're a little puzzled. This book will help you decide if being a vegetarian is the lifestyle for you and if so, how to pursue it.

The old myth that vegetarians are not as healthy as other individuals is no longer accepted, as you'll read later on. In fact, studies show that vegetarians live longer and healthier lives than people who eat meat. If you do your nutrition homework and eat correctly, you will get just as many vitamins and nutrients as anyone who eats meat, if not more. By learning about appropriate vegetarian substitutes for meat and other animal products, even young children and growing teenagers can choose vegetarianism as a healthy lifestyle.

Vegetarian Food

As more and more people have become vegetarians, the quality of the food available to vegetarians has improved. Many mainstream restaurants now offer a range of vegetarian meals. Even a few fast-food restaurants offer non-meat choices, such as veggie burgers.

Advertisements and TV commercials show families eating meatless burgers and vegetable breakfast patties made by some of the country's foremost food manufacturers, including Green Giant. Airlines make vegetarian meals available to passengers, and many coffee shops provide soy milk for those who avoid dairy products.

Today's conveniences, such as microwave ovens and prepackaged foods, make cooking vegetarian food at home easier than ever. Rice and potatoes, which used to require lengthy cooking times on the stove or in the oven, can now be ready in minutes in the microwave. You can buy numerous kinds of frozen vegetable dishes, meatless pizzas, vegetarian burritos, and veggie burgers in your local grocery store that taste delicious.

Most people still have some misconceptions about what a vegetarian is. Television and movies like to portray vegetarians as crazy hippies who belong to cults or live offbeat lifestyles, such as Dharma and her friends on the popular TV show *Dharma & Greg.* But as you'll discover in this book, most vegetarians live just like everyone else except that they don't eat meat.

As you read on, you will learn that there are several types of vegetarians and many reasons why people decide not to eat meat. You'll discover many ways to take the first steps toward eliminating meat from your diet and find suggestions for meat-free meals. Most teenagers opt to make their transition to a meat-free diet gradual, eliminating red meat first, then poultry, then seafood. Some choose to go further and eventually give up dairy foods, eggs, and other animal products.

If you are seriously considering becoming a vegetarian,

There are more food choices for vegetarians than ever before.

do your research so that you can make your decision wisely. Be sure to tell your friends and family about your choice so that they will understand your needs and support you. You will find that making the choice to be a vegetarian is a decision for which your body will thank you for the rest of your life.

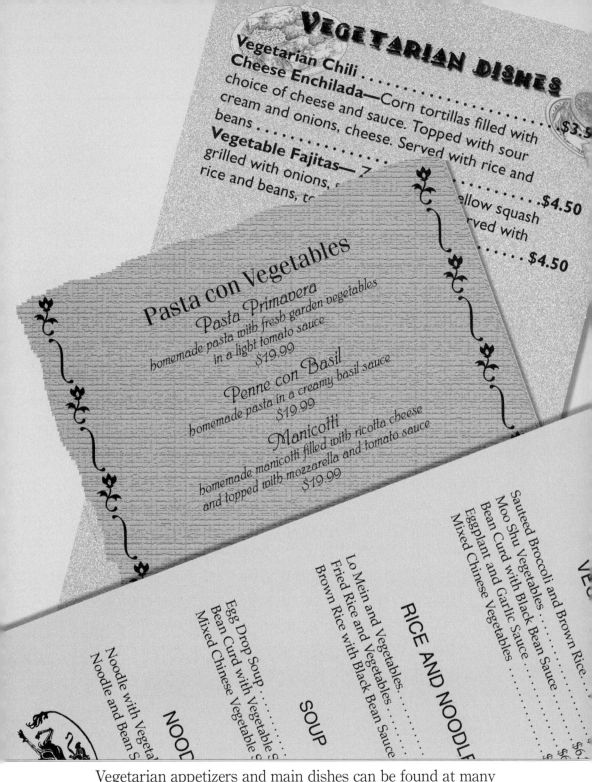

VEGETARIAN DISHES

Vegetarian Chili $3.5

Cheese Enchilada—Corn tortillas filled with choice of cheese and sauce. Topped with sour cream and onions, cheese. Served with rice and beans $4.50

Vegetable Fajitas— 7 . . . . grilled with onions, ... ellow squash rice and beans, t . . . . rved with $4.50

Pasta con Vegetables

Pasta Primavera
homemade pasta with fresh garden vegetables
in a light tomato sauce
$19.99

Penne con Basil
homemade pasta in a creamy basil sauce
$19.99

Manicotti
homemade manicotti filled with ricotta cheese
and topped with mozzarella and tomato sauce
$19.99

Sauteed Broccoli and Brown Rice $6
Moo Shu Vegetables . . . .
Bean Curd with Garlic Sauce . . . .
Eggplant and Vegetables
Mixed Chinese Vegetables

VE

RICE AND NOODL

Lo Mein and Vegetables . . . .
Fried Rice and Vegetables . . . .
Brown Rice with Black Bean Sauce

SOUP

Egg Drop Soup . . . . Vegetable S
Bean Curd with Vegetable
Mixed Chinese Vegetable S

NOODL

Noodle with Veget
Noodle and Bean S

Vegetarian appetizers and main dishes can be found at many different types of restaurants.

Chapter 1

What and Who Are Vegetarians?

In simple terms, a vegetarian is someone who does not eat meat or any kind of animal flesh. Today vegetarians fall into three categories. People in the first category, which is also the most strict, are called vegans. Vegans do not eat any animal products at all, including dairy foods, eggs, or even honey. Most vegans also avoid using animal products such as wool and leather. Becoming a vegan can be difficult for many people. Even if you find that it's easy enough to cut out foods such as omelets and yogurt from your diet, you will soon discover that many of your favorite foods, including bread, cake, and pasta, may contain eggs, butter, or other animal products.

If you currently eat meat, you may find it easier to try one of the other, more common forms of vegetarianism. Ovo-lacto vegetarians eat no animal flesh but do eat both eggs and dairy products. This is probably the most common type of vegetarianism. Lacto vegetarians eat no meat or eggs but do eat dairy products. These names come from the Latin words for egg (*ovum*) and milk (*lac*).

Who *Isn't* a Vegetarian

If you talk to people about your interest in vegetarianism, you may hear someone tell you that he or she is a vegetarian but eats fish and/or chicken. In truth these people are not vegetarians. Many people give up red meat—beef, pork, and lamb—as a first step toward becoming vegetarians, but since fish and birds (chickens, turkeys, ducks, etc.) are animals, no one who eats their flesh can be called a vegetarian.

Hidden Ingredients

People who are trying to become vegetarians don't often realize how many foods contain animal products. Gelatin, for example, is a substance made from animal bones, and true vegetarians do not eat it. Giving up gelatin may not sound like a big deal, but if you look at labels, you'll find that it is an ingredient in many vitamins, candies, and desserts, including marshmallows. Animal shortening, or lard, is another ingredient that appears in surprising places, including many types of cookies.

Fortunately it's getting easier to find an alternative to a food that contains animal ingredients. You can find agar, an animal-free alternative to gelatin, at many health food stores, and some kosher gelatin is not made from animal bones. If you become a vegetarian, make sure you read the labels on everything you buy. Ask the store clerk for help if you are unsure about a particular ingredient, or contact one of the resources listed at the end of this book.

A Long History

Vegetarianism is not new. It's not an untested trend that will go out of style. The history of vegetarianism goes back to ancient Indian and Greek civilizations. The philosopher Pythagoras, born in approximately 580 BC, believed in and recommended a vegetarian diet. (You may remember him from the Pythagorean theorem, which you've probably studied in math class.) His teachings influenced his fellow philosophers Socrates and Plato, who also declared the virtues of a vegetarian lifestyle. When the Romans came into power, eating meat became fashionable again; they enjoyed feasting on animal foods such as fish and poultry. It was not until the fifth century AD that vegetarianism became popular again.

During the fifteenth century, painter, sculptor, and inventor Leonardo da Vinci (1452–1519) was one of the most notable vegetarians in Western society. Da Vinci believed that using animals for clothing and food was brutal and showed a lack of mercy. Da Vinci also rejected the idea of using any animal products for food or clothing. (In this way, he was similar to today's vegans, about whom you will learn more later.)

The vegetarian movement that exists today has its roots in the nineteenth century. During that time another great artist, the playwright George Bernard Shaw (1856–1950), was a prominent vegetarian. He became a vegetarian in his early twenties and remained one until he died at age ninety-four.

The vegetarian movement experienced another "comeback" in the 1960s. This was a time of protest and upheaval in many parts of the world, but it also brought a great many positive changes in the rights of women and minorities. In Western society, along with the call for an end to the war in Vietnam came a call for people to care for the environment and the world around us. Many of the people who were active in this new environmental movement were vegetarians. Health food stores and vegetarian restaurants began to appear in some cities and many college towns around the United States.

Famous Vegetarians

You have already heard about a few of history's best-known vegetarians; some others you might be familiar with include William Shakespeare, Thomas Edison, Albert Einstein, and Mary Wollstonecraft Shelley, author of *Frankenstein.* Today an even greater number of successful artists, athletes, and scholars promote the benefits of a vegetarian lifestyle.

Some of our greatest athletes are vegetarians. These include tennis champion Martina Navratilova, baseball

Paul McCartney and his late wife, Linda, started an all-vegetarian frozen-food company as part of the McCartneys' advocacy of a vegetarian lifestyle.

player and home run champion Hank Aaron, and Kathy Johnson, an Olympic medalist in gymnastics. They and other great athletes are living proof that vegetarians are not weaker and less active than those who eat meat, as some claim they are. Movie and television stars like Steve Martin, Dustin Hoffman, Kim Basinger, and Sara Gilbert are all proudly vegetarian. Maybe you've danced to the music of Michael Jackson, Natalie Merchant, or Paul McCartney, all of whom are vegetarians as well.

Chapter 2

Why Be a Vegetarian?

P eople choose to become vegetarians for a variety of reasons. Some people believe that it is wrong to kill animals for food or to graze them on land that could be used to grow crops to feed people. Others choose vegetarianism for health reasons or because of their religious beliefs. Some people just don't enjoy the taste of meat. A book, TV show, or movie might influence someone's decision to switch to a meatless diet. For many people it's a combination of reasons.

You are not alone if you are considering vegetarianism at this point in your life. Many people make the switch to vegetarianism as teenagers. As a young adult, you are beginning to take responsibility for your own life. You are developing your own opinions about lifestyle choices and following your own tastes in food. You are learning more about the world around you and realizing that your actions directly affect the earth. For many teenagers, not eating meat is one of those actions that can have a positive effect.

Some common reasons that people give for making the switch to vegetarianism are listed below.

Love of Animals and a Belief in Animal Rights

Often people who grew up with animals as pets feel that the killing of animals is wrong. As children we are taught to love all animals, and we usually think they are cute. Children may not realize that a hamburger is made from the cow they see grazing in the field, or that a chicken nugget was once a real chicken like the ones at the farm their class visited. Many adults, children, and teens who are longtime meat eaters are turned off by meat once they begin to associate it with a favorite animal. Even a movie like *Babe,* the story of an adorable pig who has endearing human qualities, can influence someone to change to a vegetarian diet.

Some people who become vegetarians because they love animals still enjoy the taste of meat. Luckily they have many choices: There are meat substitutes that taste and even look like real meat, which you will read more about later.

Keisha hasn't eaten meat in years. "I never had a pet growing up," she says, "but seeing a lobster being cooked turned me off from eating any animal or fish. I knew that meats came from various animals, but I tried to disguise

Babe is a favorite film of many vegetarians.

the look and flavor of meat by always making sure that everything I ate was cooked well-done, usually to the point of being charred. But one day, my parents brought home some fresh lobsters from the fish store for dinner. We let the lobsters crawl around on our patio and had fun naming them and watching them interact with each other. When it was time to cook them, I saw these creatures that I had just played with being thrown alive into a pot of boiling water. I couldn't eat that night, and that was when I became interested in vegetarianism."

Ethics

Ethical concerns often go hand in hand with a love of animals. People who become vegetarians for ethical reasons have a problem not only with killing animals for food but also with the cruel way that these animals are raised and slaughtered.

Over seven billion animals are killed for food each year, and these animals usually live in bleak conditions. Owners of large factory farms, who are interested mainly in making a profit, keep livestock in overcrowded buildings to keep down the costs of housing them. The animals are not allowed to roam freely, and some are kept in cages so small that they cannot even turn around. Many animals kept in close quarters die from suffocation even before being slaughtered. Those that survive long enough to be slaughtered have led a miserable existence.

To prevent disease from spreading in the crowded buildings, animals are given antibiotics to keep them from getting sick. Farm animals are also typically given hormones to make them bigger or so that they will produce more young. These powerful substances are eaten by the animals and eventually wind up in your system if you consume the meat, eggs, or milk from one of these animals. Many people stop eating animals to avoid putting these substances into their own bodies.

If you do research, you will discover many facts about the butchering of animals for food. Be aware that although most of what you learn is true, there may also be exaggerated or false information out there that is intended to sway your feelings and opinions. Read wisely and make intelligent, well-thought-out decisions about your eating choices.

Some meat eaters prefer free-range meat. They may believe that the animals are allowed to live as normally as possible until they are slaughtered. People may also think that free-range meat is free of antibiotics and other chemicals, unlike most factory-produced meat. Many aspiring vegetarians, especially those who have become vegetarians because of ethical concerns, switch to free-range meats and eggs until they are ready to take the next step and cut meat out of their diet entirely. Unfortunately, meat companies can claim that almost any meat is free-range as long as the animal had some access to the outdoors during its life. This means that meat labeled "free-range" may be very much like factory-farmed meat. Research organic food markets in your area and always ask questions and read labels carefully.

Most people who choose vegetarianism for ethical reasons also avoid the use of animal products such as leather, wool, and feathers for clothing and household items.

Environment

Some people become vegetarians in part because they believe that raising farm animals is damaging to the environment. They believe that it would be better to use the land on which farm animals graze for growing plant crops, which could feed larger numbers of people. If the same land is used for grazing too many animals for too long, erosion and other environmental problems can result. Crop farming can also cause erosion, however, and changing grazing land to crop land would not be a simple process.

Many vegetarians oppose the use of land for the grazing of cattle and other farm animals.

This is a complicated issue, and you will find inaccurate information on both sides of the debate. If you are interested in learning about the effects of animal farming on the land, the organizations listed in Where to Go for Help can lead you to more information.

Health

Each year, more and more studies confirm the fact that eating meat and other animal products can greatly increase your chances of developing conditions such as high cholesterol, heart disease, cancer, and diabetes. Animal foods are generally high in fat, and too much fat in the diet has been linked to these problems as well as others. Fruits and vegetables, in contrast, are naturally low in fat, so eating a vegetarian or vegan diet lowers your risk of disease. In addition, many staples of a vegetarian diet, such as soy products and dark green, leafy vegetables, are high in fiber and other nutrients that are thought to actively prevent these diseases. Studies also show that on average, vegetarians live longer than those who eat meat.

"I've always been a healthy person," says Luis. "I run track at school and play on a basketball team over the summer. But sometimes after a long day at school, I felt run down and tired. Even though I had never had a problem with my weight before, when I became a teenager, my body started to show the effects of all the junk food I was eating with my friends. I also started paying attention to the news. It seemed as if almost every day, I heard something new about the health benefits of a stalk of broccoli and the harm in a hamburger. Between salmonella food poisoning and mad cow disease, not to mention all that fat, I don't see why anyone would risk his or her health for the sake of a steak. I quit eating meat about a year ago, and I've felt a lot better since then. I look a lot better, too."

Other reasons for choosing vegetarianism include being influenced by friends or people you admire, religious beliefs, or even wanting to rebel against your parents or your current lifestyle.

You may find that you are considering vegetarianism

Becoming a vegetarian is easier when you have the support of friends.

because of a combination of reasons. Maybe you have your own specific ideas about why to go meatless. The important thing is to understand why you want to make the change, learn as much as you can, and come to a conclusion for the right reasons, not just because of a TV show or a friend's influence. Once you have the facts to make an educated decision, then you can commit to it. You will find that you are not alone and that you will have support, whatever your reasons.

Chapter 3

Talking to Your Family and Friends

Once you make the decision to become a vegetarian, your next step will be speaking with your parents and your friends about how your eating habits—and in many ways, your life—will change.

Your Family

Before you decide to tell your parents about your decision, make sure you have stocked up on information so that you can approach them with all the details at hand. They might think that you are just going through a phase. They might wonder which of your friends is a vegetarian and whom you are trying to emulate. They might not know exactly what a vegetarian is, or they might think that giving up meat will be bad for your health. It is up to you to give them the lowdown on what vegetarianism is, why you are becoming one, and most importantly, what you are going to eat.

Your parents are concerned about your health, and you need to assure them that you understand what kind of responsibility you are taking on. Your parents will be more likely to support you in this decision if you show them that you will play an active role in eating right and staying healthy. Show them some recipes. Offer to cook a vegetarian meal for the family so they can see the healthy varieties of food you will be eating. Spend time cooking or shopping with them so they will know what they should stock the kitchen with. Agree to talk to your family physician about the best ways to get the vitamins and nutrients that a growing teenager needs.

"I was never a big meat eater, so when I told my mother that I was going to be a vegetarian, she wasn't surprised," says Rebekah. *"She wanted to know how she could be supportive. At first she was concerned about my getting enough protein, and she kept suggesting that I eat at least some fish or an omelet. But once she realized that I was serious about not eating anything that came from an animal, she decided to take an active role. She started coming home with new foods for me to try, taking me to the natural food markets, and cutting out newspaper articles about vegetarianism and nutrition for me to read."*

Your parents may know what vegetarianism is, but they are probably unfamiliar with veganism. If you

Help your family to understand your nutritional needs as a
vegetarian by taking an active role in food shopping.

choose a vegan lifestyle, it may be difficult for your family to understand your refusal to do certain things, like taking vitamins made with gelatin or wearing leather. As you learn more about vegetarianism and the treatment of animals, you might even start to resent your parents for their food and lifestyle choices. It's fine to let them know how you feel about your mother's fur coat or your father's love of veal, but don't lecture or preach to them. You will make a bigger impact by setting an example and slowly introducing your parents to new foods and ideas.

Friends

You may get a similar reaction from your friends. They might accuse you of trying to be like your favorite movie star or of simply wanting attention. Or they might just not understand why you can't have marshmallows in your hot chocolate.

Kevin became a vegan about a year ago. "At first it was difficult to explain to my friends," he says. "They kept talking about all the things I couldn't eat. They reminded me of how much I was going to miss eating tacos and chicken cutlets. At first it was really hard to see my friends eating hot dogs at baseball games and pizza at sleepovers while I was picking at lettuce and carrots. But then it became kind of fun. I always had something to talk about at parties or at restaurants, and I was often the center of attention!"

Being around your nonvegetarian friends may be hard at first.

You would not want your friends lecturing you on what to eat, and it's important for you to be accepting of their choices as well. They will probably be curious about your new habits. Share information with them; stand up for what you believe in; and direct them to Web sites, support groups, or books to answer their questions. If you are disapproving or condescending toward them, they will likely become turned off about vegetarianism—and about you.

It is also possible that your friends will share your interest in vegetarianism. Some of them may be vegetarians themselves. If that's the case, you can share tips and ideas about meals to eat, restaurants to visit, and ways to encourage others to eat a meatless diet. You can have fun cooking meals together too.

Chapter 4

How to Get Started

Once your family and friends quiz you about why you are choosing this lifestyle, the next question you will hear is, "But what will you eat?!" Get used to it. Chances are you will be answering this question for the rest of your life.

Don't worry. It's not all seaweed and salad, if that's what you are thinking. What you and many other people may not realize is how much vegetarian food you already eat. How many times this month have you had pizza, spaghetti with tomato sauce, or macaroni and cheese? What about corn on the cob or a baked potato? You have probably tried a bean burrito or a veggie spring roll at some point, too. Once you start to count the vegetarian choices that are already part of your diet, you will realize that being a vegetarian is a lot easier than you thought.

Soy protein comes in many versatile forms, such as tempeh.

Beyond Vegetables

It makes sense that vegetarians eat lots of vegetables. But what else do they eat? When you start exploring the world of vegetarianism, you'll probably come across some foods that you have never heard of. These might include the following:

Soy

Soy is an inexpensive, easily available food that comes from soybeans. It is also a great source of protein, fiber, and cancer-fighting nutrients. Soy comes in many forms and can be used in everything from soups and main dishes to shakes and desserts.

The most popular form of soy is bean curd, or tofu.

Tofu is soft and white and is usually sold in cubes. It has the texture of a soft cheese. Tofu doesn't have much flavor of its own, but it takes on the taste of whatever you cook it with. Throw it into a stir-fry with soy sauce, ginger, garlic, and veggies. Blend some soft tofu into a creamy salad dressing. Many popular types of veggie burgers are made with tofu. If you have ever had Chinese, Thai, or Japanese food, you've probably already had tofu without even knowing it, because it is used as an ingredient in many soups and main dishes.

A less common (but equally delicious) form of soy is tempeh, made from fermented soybeans. Tempeh is denser than tofu and has a texture and taste similar to that of meat. Many people choose to use tempeh in vegetarian versions of meat dishes. Tempeh and other soy products, such as texturized soy protein, are used in making many of the meat substitutes on the market. These substitutes are designed with the look and taste of meats such as chicken, turkey, and sausage.

Whole soybeans are a great alternative to snack foods like popcorn. Buy them frozen at any whole-food market or health food store (where they're usually called *eda-mame*), and boil them in salted water for an appetizer. Roasted soybeans are called soy nuts and are another healthy, crunchy snack.

Grains

Grains—foods such as rice, oats, wheat, and barley—are another staple of a vegetarian diet. They probably

Vegetarians have an amazing number of versatile grains from which to choose.

make up a large part of your diet already. Foods like oatmeal, bread, pasta, and cereal are all made from grains. Whole-grain foods, such as brown rice and whole-wheat bread, are healthier and more satisfying than foods made from processed grains, such as white rice and white bread.

There are also many types of grains that you may not yet be familiar with, such as millet, amaranth, and quinoa. Try these for a healthy and delicious change.

Dairy Product Alternatives

If you have chosen to become a vegan and are eliminating dairy products, you will be happy to know that you don't need to give up foods like pizza, cheese burritos,

There are many protein sources and dairy alternatives available to vegetarians and vegans.

or even cereal with milk. There are lots of alternatives to traditional dairy products.

Soy milk is one of a vegan's best substitutes. Many people find that vanilla-flavored soy milk tastes better than other flavors. You can use soy milk in coffee; in your cereal; or blended with frozen bananas, strawberries, and apple juice for a sweet, creamy smoothie. Many vegetarians also like rice milk or nut milk, which taste similar to real milk and are not as thick in consistency as soy milk.

Soy cheese is a popular dairy alternative as well. Soy cheese is delicious and melts just as easily as cheese made from cow's milk. Like regular cheese, soy cheese comes in many different varieties, such as Monterey

Jack for Mexican dishes and American for a great grilled-cheese sandwich.

Ethnic Food

One of the easiest ways to find vegetarian dishes is to try eating foods from other countries and cultures. Whereas the typical American diet is usually meat based, including foods such as hamburgers, meatloaf, and pot roast, you can find plenty of delicious meatless meals on ethnic menus. Try visiting some local ethnic restaurants, or experiment with ethnic cooking by finding cookbooks at the library. Here are some ideas to get you started:

- **Asian Food:** Asian cooking offers numerous choices for vegetarians and vegans. Many Chinese, Thai, Korean, and Japanese main courses contain tofu, and soy products and rice have historically played a role in Asian cooking. There are also a variety of sautéed vegetables and noodles that can be prepared in endless ways. Moo shu vegetables are sautéed and served in thin pancakes topped with plum sauce. Cold sesame noodles have a spicy peanut sauce. At a Japanese restaurant, vegetable tempura is always a great choice. Indian food is also a good option for vegetarians. In some areas of India, meat is not eaten at all. Vegetables, rice, and legumes such as lentils and chickpeas are the basis for many Indian dishes. Indian food is often heavily

Italian cuisine provides many delicious food options for vegetarians.

spiced with various curries and other seasonings that make the dish more flavorful and satisfying, even without meat.

• **Italian Food:** The obvious choice here is pasta, and again you'll have plenty of options. Even if you are eliminating dairy from your diet, you can still have your pasta served with tomato sauce, with garlic and oil, or primavera (with vegetables). A simple plate of grilled vegetables drizzled with olive oil is another staple of Italian cooking. And almost any restaurant will make you a cheeseless pizza piled high with vegetables and tomato sauce.

• **Middle Eastern Food:** Hummus, falafel, and baba ganoush: These may seem like unfamiliar names to you now, but eventually you will realize that these are common foods—and delicious ones. Both falafel and hummus are just ground, flavored chickpeas prepared in different ways, and baba ganoush is made from pureed eggplant. Middle Eastern cuisine offers many other vegetarian options as well.

• **Mexican Food:** This is another great food option for vegetarians. Think of all the delicious choices: black beans and rice, bean burritos, and guacamole, to name just a few. But be aware that seemingly vegetarian options like refried beans

Guacamole, an avocado-based dip, is a vegetarian favorite.

may contain meat or be cooked with animal fat.
Be sure to ask before you order.

These are just a few of the opportunities to eat new
foods that being a vegetarian gives you. Your worst problem will be deciding what to try first! You will come to
realize how many vegetarian options your favorite restaurants (even fast-food and chain restaurants) offer. Instead
of a turkey sandwich at the deli, have a veggie burger or
a sandwich of lettuce, tomatoes, and sprouts (and cheese,
if you eat it). For a change from peanut butter and jelly,
try some soy nut butter. At baseball games, opt for
nachos and salsa instead of a hot dog. Are Mom and Dad
grilling steaks for dinner? Why not brush some firm tofu

Vegetarianism can open you up to a whole new world of food and cooking options.

with barbecue sauce and grill it? Have you ever tried a stuffed artichoke or a black-bean burrito? As you familiarize yourself with vegetarianism, you will find new ways of combining foods that you already love in order to make interesting dishes. Your family may find your new eating habits strange, but in time they may become curious and join you as you try new foods.

Take the initiative: Go shopping with your parents and stock up on frozen meals and foods that you can prepare on your own. Spend a Saturday afternoon making casseroles and soups that you can refrigerate or freeze for future meals. Your family will see how passionate you are about your new lifestyle and will be much more interested in trying the foods you introduce them to.

Chapter 5

Nutrition and Staying Healthy

Even if you have convinced them that being a vegetarian is right for you, your parents may still have concerns about your health, and you might too. How will you grow up strong and healthy? How will you have the energy to run track or play on the football team? These are valid questions, but in fact, vegetarians are some of the healthiest people around.

Vegetarians do have to pay attention to what they eat, and vegans have to be especially sure that they are getting the right amounts of nutrients. You would not expect to stay healthy if you ate nothing but pizza, french fries, and cookies, and this is true for vegetarians as much as for meat eaters.

Vegetarian Myths

More and more people are giving up meat, but many

It is not hard for vegetarians to get all the protein they need.

people still believe that vegetarianism leads to poor health. They will tell you that your bones will get weak because you're not drinking milk or that you will have no energy if you don't get protein from meat. The following are some of the nutrients that you will hear about:

- **Protein:** A question you'll soon get tired of hearing is, "But how do you get enough protein if you don't eat meat?" This is one of the biggest misconceptions about a vegetarian diet. All of the protein you need can be found in beans, nuts, grains, and soy products. Some studies say that when these foods are eaten in combination with the

right starches— for example, beans with brown
rice or peanut butter on whole-grain bread—our
bodies are able to use these proteins more easily
than meat protein. The average vegetarian con-
sumes more than enough protein to be healthy.

• **Calcium:** Another common myth is that vegetarians, especially vegans, do not get enough
calcium because they do not drink milk or eat
dairy products. Dairy products are a popular
source of calcium, but they may not be the best
source, especially since they are often high in fat.
If you are a vegan, you do have to be extra-care-
ful to get the calcium you need, but there are
plenty of ways to get it. Dark green, leafy vegetables like spinach, kale, and broccoli are excel-
lent sources of calcium. Calcium is also found in
foods such as winter squash, almonds, and some
beans. Most soy and rice beverages, along with
tofu and some brands of orange juice, have extra
calcium added.

• **Iron:** Iron is an important nutrient that helps
carry oxygen to the blood. Iron deficiency has
long been one of the main concerns for vegetarians because the body absorbs the iron from
red meat faster than the iron from plants. But
adding vitamin C to the diet helps your body
absorb iron from plants, so this problem is easy

Vegetarians and vegans should eat lots of dark green leafy vegetables to get a sufficient amount of calcium.

to fix. To get iron, vegetarians choose foods like dried fruits (raisins and prunes are a great and easy choice), dark leafy greens, legumes, and grains. Adding foods rich in vitamin C to your diet has other health benefits too. Because women lose iron during menstruation, female vegetarians have to be extra-cautious about getting enough iron and should consider taking iron supplements. Check with your doctor if you are not sure that you are getting the iron you need.

- **Vitamin B$_{12}$:** Vitamin B$_{12}$ is found only in various animal products. Too little of this vitamin can cause fatigue, nerve damage, and certain kinds of anemia (a blood disorder). If you eat an ovo-lacto vegetarian diet, you will get more than enough of this nutrient. Also, it is believed that vitamin B_{12} is retained in our bodies for long periods of time, so if you have eaten animal products in the past, you should have enough of this nutrient to last for several years. However, it is often recommended that vegetarians and especially vegans take a B_{12} supplement or eat cereals fortified with B_{12} to ensure good health.

If you are careful to plan your diet so that it includes enough of these and other important nutrients—like zinc, vitamin D, and fiber, for example—you will be as healthy as, or more healthy than, most meat eaters.

The Road to Better Health

A vegetarian diet can help prevent or combat many diseases, including the following:

- **Cancer:** A diet high in fat is thought to be one of the leading causes of cancer. Vegetarians tend to eat less fat than those who eat meat, and they also consume more carotene, a nutrient believed to be a defense against cancer. Carotene is found in fruits and vegetables such as carrots, mangoes, and sweet potatoes. A vegetarian diet can reduce the risk of cancers such as skin, stomach, and colon cancer.

- **Heart Disease:** Eating a diet high in two types of fat, saturated fat and cholesterol, increases the chance of heart disease. A vegetarian diet, which puts an emphasis on fiber and carbohydrates, can help to prevent heart trouble by lowering your intake of fat and reducing the cholesterol in your body.

- **Diabetes:** The bodies of people with diabetes do not produce enough insulin, a substance that controls the level of sugar in the blood. Studies have shown that a vegetarian diet can help prevent diabetes. Beans and other types of legumes help control the blood-sugar level, so that the body needs to produce less insulin to stabilize itself.

If you are seriously considering vegetarianism and have any health problems at all, you should check with your family doctor before changing your diet. If you plan correctly, you won't need additional vitamin supplements; however, your doctor can make suggestions to help ensure your good health and to ease the worries of your family.

Even with all the information you now have, your parents may still be unwilling to let you stop eating meat. Since your parents most likely pay for the food that you eat, you will have to respect their rules and decisions about what you eat. If you cannot be a vegetarian at home, you may still want to follow a meatless diet when

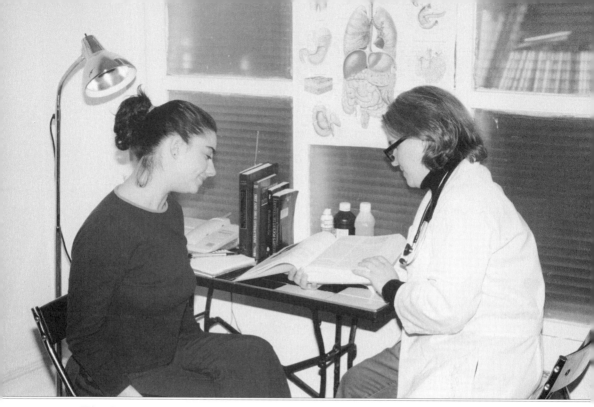

The health benefits of a vegetarian diet are well documented.

you are at school or when you buy food with your own money. Make sure to tell your parents what you have learned about vegetarianism, and if you know another adult who is vegetarian, consider having him or her talk to your parents too. It may take time, but if they know the facts and understand that you are serious, most parents will likely agree to let their kids try vegetarianism.

Chapter 6

Special Occasions

In general, most vegetarians do not have too much trouble giving up meat. They don't miss the taste of meat for long, and they find great alternatives to make their meals tasty and interesting. But many agree that difficulties can arise when they leave their houses and enter a world that is not tailored to a vegetarian lifestyle. You will encounter many challenges if you decide to become a vegetarian, from what to do when your friends want pepperoni on their pizza to how to handle holiday meals. Fortunately, though, with a little bit of creativity, you can almost always find solutions.

School Functions

What do you do after a basketball game when your coach takes the team to McDonald's to celebrate? How

Bringing a vegetarian dish when visiting friends can help to
make eating at others' homes more comfortable.

do you handle a class barbecue, a school lunch, or dinner before the prom?

Relax—it all sounds more difficult than it is. Believe it or not, most schools will cater to your needs. Increasingly, high schools and colleges are offering vegetarian meals for students. You may find that you are not the only one making a special request; you may have classmates who need kosher or halal meals (prepared according to Jewish or Islamic dietary laws) or require specific foods for health reasons. There may even be another vegetarian like you.

More and more school cafeterias offer at least one vegetarian choice each day, such as meatless pasta or pizza. If your school's cafeteria isn't veggie-friendly, try talking to the principal to see if the menu can be changed, or bring lunch from home. Almost any cafeteria or restaurant will make you a peanut butter and jelly sandwich. If it's a more formal occasion like an awards dinner, a school dance, or the prom, ask the waiter to put together a vegetable plate made up of the side dishes for the meat entrees. You will probably get a plate of potatoes, carrots, broccoli, and corn, and it may be fresher and more appetizing than the meals that your classmates are eating!

Dinner at a Friend's House

Eating at a friend's house can be difficult and uncomfortable, especially if you're worried about inconveniencing or insulting your host. Often it is better to let your friends (and their parents) know in advance that you don't eat meat. That way they can make sure to have enough vegetables, side dishes, and bread on hand to fill you up. Many vegetarian meals are easy to prepare, and your host will probably not mind boiling some pasta and adding canned tomato sauce. You can also make the experience easier by offering to bring a salad, an appetizer, or even a vegetarian main dish for everyone to try. In this way, you can remind your host of your dietary needs and help out. Some hosts may still see your vegetarianism as a problem, but the more solutions you can provide in advance, the more acccpting they are likely to be.

"I hate to make a fuss when I go to a friend's house for dinner," says Keisha. *"I'm lucky that most of my friends know about my diet, so they will ask their parents to make a separate dish for me or order half the pizza without pepperoni. If that doesn't work, I'm careful to assure my friends' parents that it's not a problem if they are having chicken cutlets; I am totally happy filling up on the bread, the side dishes, and the salad. If I know enough in advance about the dinner plans, I'll bring along a dip like hummus or guacamole for everyone to enjoy. That's a good way to make sure that there is at least one thing I can eat!"*

Holidays

Many vegetarians will tell you that they never had a problem making the transition to meatlessness until a

Tofu "turkeys" with all the trimmings are one interesting vegetarian alternative to the traditional holiday meal.

holiday like Thanksgiving came along. It wasn't just the turkey they couldn't eat but also the stuffing and the gravy. You may have to forgo the turkey on Thanksgiving, but between the potatoes, squash, corn, and dozens of vegetables to choose from, you will have a feast. If you are going to a friend's or relative's house, you may want let them know that you plan to bring a frozen veggie burger or burrito just in case. That way, it is less likely that your hosts will be offended, and it will make them feel less anxiety about having to prepare something special for you. Also, there are some fantastic holiday cookbooks for vegetarians, so if you like to cook, you can try making your own turkey-free feast.

Vacations

When you are on vacation, finding the best places to eat vegetarian meals can be tricky. Again, though, most restaurants will be happy to accommodate your request for a simple plate of vegetables, and many offer at least one vegetarian choice. If you are traveling in a foreign country where you don't speak the language, it can be a little more difficult, so be prepared to eat basic foods like bread and potatoes. Many travel guides list restaurants that offer vegetarian meals, and there are even guides specifically aimed at vegetarian travelers. Bring along a dictionary or phrase book so that you can look up the words for particular ingredients in dishes. Airline food has a bad reputation, but major airlines offer surprisingly good vegetarian meals. Just remember to order the vegetarian selection at least twenty-four hours in advance.

"When I went to Europe, I found that some countries had terrific vegetarian choices," says Luis. "The Burger King in England had veggie burgers, and the pasta in Italy was fantastic. But in other countries, vegetarian meals meant soggy broccoli and french fries. Even foods that I was familiar with, like beans or soups, were often made with meat. In the countries where I didn't speak the language, it often seemed safest just to order the potatoes. But I found that if I asked the hotel staff or looked through guidebooks, I could always find a place to get some great vegetarian food."

Chapter 7

Sample Recipes and Meal Ideas

By now you are probably thinking, "This all sounds great . . . but what will I really eat? What will a typical day's menu look like? Won't it get boring eating different combinations of beans and spinach every day?"

To ease your fears, here are some basic vegetarian recipes and meal ideas to get you started. Try some of these conventional recipes and then venture on to more daring fare like tempeh and seitan (made from wheat). Buy some vegetarian cookbooks. Eat at vegetarian restaurants and get some ideas from the menus there. Be creative. You will soon find that you have so many options to choose from that you won't miss meat at all.

Hummus (vegan)
- 1 15 oz. can of chickpeas, drained and rinsed
- 2 tablespoons of extra virgin olive oil

Hummus is a staple of many vegetarian diets.

- 2 cloves of garlic, chopped
- 2 tablespoons of fresh lemon juice
- 2 tablespoons of tahini (sesame butter)
- 1 teaspoon of ground cumin
- Pinch of ground coriander
- 4 tablespoons of chopped parsley
- 1/2 teaspoon of salt

1. Place all ingredients into a blender and puree until smooth. If the mixture is too thick to blend, add small amounts of water until it is thin enough.
2. Scoop out with a spatula and serve cold as a dip with warm pita bread or fresh, cut vegetables. (Hummus also makes a great sandwich filling. Just

spread it generously on your choice of bread; add some lettuce, tomato, and sprouts; and you're ready to go!)

Vegetable Puree Soup (vegan)

(This is one of the fastest, easiest soups to make, and you can modify it to your own taste!)

- 1/2 of an onion, peeled and diced.
- 2 cloves of garlic, chopped.
- 2 teaspoons of olive oil.
- 1 large russet potato, peeled and cubed.
- 3 cups of vegetable broth.
- 3 cups of water.
- 2 cups of cut broccoli (fresh or frozen).
- 1 cup of peeled, cut carrots (fresh or frozen).
- 1 cup of spinach (fresh or frozen).
- Other vegetables, such as mushrooms, corn, or cauliflower—add as many as you want according to taste.
- Salt and pepper to taste.

1. In a large saucepan, combine the vegetable broth, water, and potato. Boil until the potatoes are soft.
2. In a large skillet, sauté the onion and garlic in olive oil.
3. Add the remaining vegetables to the sauté and cook over low heat until all vegetables are soft and thoroughly cooked.

4. Add the vegetable sauté to the potato/vegetable broth mixture. Let simmer for 5 minutes.
5. Put the entire vegetable mixture into a blender and puree until creamy. Add salt and pepper to taste and garnish with croutons or whole-grain crackers.

Tofu-Vegetable Stir-Fry (vegan)

- 1 14 oz. package of firm tofu, drained and cut into bite-size cubes.
- 3 cups of fresh or frozen vegetables. (Again, feel free to add the vegetables you like. The frozen food section of most supermarkets offers a ready-made stir-fry vegetable packet with goodies like water chestnuts, baby corn, and snow peas, as well as broccoli and carrots.)
- 4 tablespoons of soy sauce.
- 2-3 tablespoons of sesame oil.
- 2 cloves of garlic.
- 1 tablespoon of chopped, fresh ginger or ginger powder.
- 2 tablespoons of plum sauce or duck sauce.

1. In a wok (or large nonstick frying pan), sauté the garlic and ginger in the sesame oil on high heat. Lower the heat and add plum or soy sauce.
2. Add the vegetables. (If using frozen vegetables, it helps to defrost them in the microwave first.)
3. Simmer for 2-3 minutes or until almost fully cooked. Add the tofu; cook on low heat for approximately 1

minute, stirring the mixture until the vegetables are fully done and the tofu has sufficiently soaked in the juices.

4. Serve hot, by itself or over brown rice.

Vanilla Fruit Smoothie

- 1/2 cup of vanilla-flavored rice or soy milk
- 1/4 cup of apple juice
- 1 whole frozen banana
- 1/4 cup of blueberries, frozen
- 1/4 cup of strawberries, frozen

1. Put all ingredients into a blender and blend until smooth. Add juice as needed if the drink is too thick.
2. Pour into glasses and serve immediately. Makes about 2 smoothies.

When you start cooking, remember to have fun. This may be your first time using the stove, but don't feel stressed out. Invent your own recipes with foods you like. Or even easier, try making familiar foods like a baked potato with melted soy cheese and broccoli. Or steamed butternut squash flavored with brown sugar or salt and pepper. Be creative about trying new things, and stick with it. Good luck and enjoy your healthy new diet!

Glossary

activist Someone who takes a direct action to
  achieve a political or social reform.
anemia A condition that affects red blood cells.
  Anemia is generally caused by nutritional problems
  such as too little iron in the diet. People with anemia are sometimes pale and weak.
calcium A substance that is needed for the develop-
  ment and maintenance of healthy bones. Calcium is
  found in dairy products and dark green vegetables.
carbohydrate An essential nutrient that we get from
  many foods, including fruits, vegetables, and grains.
carotene A nutrient that is found in many fruits and
  vegetables and is believed to help prevent some
  types of cancer.
cholesterol A substance that occurs naturally in our
  bodies and is also found in certain foods. A high
  level of cholesterol in the body can lead to heart
  disease and other health problems.
factory farm A large farming operation, usually
  owned by a company rather than an individual,
  that produces very large quantities of farm products. Most of the meat and dairy products sold in
  the United States are produced by factory farms.

fiber A substance found in some foods that helps keep the digestive system healthy.

free-range Taken from an animal that was allowed access to the outdoors rather than being kept in a cage.

lacto vegetarian Someone who does not eat animal flesh but does eat dairy products.

legumes A group of plant foods that includes peas, beans, and peanuts.

nutrient A substance found in food that helps our bodies remain healthy.

ovo-lacto vegetarian Someone who does not eat animal flesh but does eat dairy products and eggs as well as foods containing those ingredients.

protein An essential nutrient that we get from certain foods, including meat, dairy products, tofu, and beans.

seitan A mixture of wheat flour, vegetable extracts, and seasonings that is used as a meat substitute.

tempeh Fermented soy with a texture similar to meat and a nutty flavor.

tofu A food made from soybeans that has a soft, cheeselike texture. Also called bean curd.

vegan A type of vegetarian who eats no animal foods or animal products such as dairy or eggs. Most vegans also abstain from using any animal products, such as feathers, wool, silk, and leather.

vitamin A type of nutrient that is essential to good health.

For Further Reading

Boyd, Billy Ray. *For the Vegetarian in You.* Rocklin, CA: Prima Publishing, 1995.

Davis, Gail. *So Now What Do I Eat? The Complete Guide to Vegetarian Convenience Foods.* Corrales, NM: Blue Coyote Press, 1998.

Ferber, Elizabeth. *The Vegetarian Life: How to Be a Veggie in a Meat-Eating World.* New York: Berkley Publishing, 1998.

Gellatley, Juliet. *The Livewire Guide to Going, Being, and Staying Veggie!* North Pomfret, VT: Trafalgar Square, 1997.

Klavan, Ellen. *The Vegetarian Factfinder.* New York: Little Bookroom, 1996.

Null, Gary. *The Vegetarian Handbook.* New York: St. Martin's Press, 1996.

Stepaniak, Joanne. *The Vegan Sourcebook.* Los Angeles: Lowell House, 1998.

Vegetarian Times. *Vegetarian Times Vegetarian Beginner's Guide.* New York: Macmillan, 1996.

Wasserman, Debra, and Reed Mangels. *Simply Vegan: Quick Vegetarian Meals.* Baltimore, MD: The Vegetarian Resource Group, 1995.

Weiss, Stefanie Iris. *Everything You Need to Know About Being a Vegan.* New York: Rosen Publishing Group, 1999.

Where to Go for Help

In the United States

The American Vegan Society
501 Old Harding Highway
Malaga, NJ 08328
609-694-2887

North American Vegetarian Society
P.O. Box 72
Dolgeville, NY 13329
(518) 568-7970
e-mail: navs@telenet.net
Web site: http://www.cyberveg.navs
Provides up-to-date information on vegetarianism and publishes *Vegetarian Voice* magazine. This organization will also help you with restaurant guides.

Vegan Action
P.O. Box 4353
Berkeley, CA 94704
(510) 548-7377
e-mail: info@vegan.org
Web site: http://www.veganorg.com

Vegetarian Awareness Network
P.O. Box 321
Knoxville, TN 37901

The Vegetarian Education Network
P.O. Box 339
Oxford, PA 19363-0339
(717) 529-8938

An organization geared toward young vegetarians. Gives advice over the phone or through their newsletter.

Vegetarian Resource Group (VRG)
P.O. Box 1463
Baltimore, MD 21203
(410) 366-8343
e-mail: vrg@vrg.org
Web site: http://www.vrg.org
Publishes the magazine *Vegetarian Journal.* VRG can help you locate vegetarian organizations in your area.

Vegetarian Union of North America
P.O. Box 9710
Washington, DC 20016
e-mail: vuna@ivu.org
Web site: http://www.ivu.org/vuna

Vegetarian Youth Network
P.O. Box 1141
New Paltz, NY 12561
Web site: http://www.geocities.com/RodeoDrive/1154
A nonprofessional organization run by teenagers for teenagers. Write to them for more information and enclose a self-addressed stamped envelope.

Veg-Teen
An on-line chat group for vegetarian teens. Join by sending an e-mail to listproc@envirolink.org.

In Canada

Canada EarthSave Society
1093 West Broadway, Suite 103
Vancouver, BC V6H 1E2
(604) 731-5885

Magazines

Vegetarian Times
For subscription information:
(800) 829-3340 or (904) 446-6914
Web site: http://www.vegetariantimes.com

Veggie Life
P.O. Box 440
Mt. Morris, IL 61054-7660
Send $23.94 for a full-year subscription. Outside of the United States, add $6.00.

Web sites

New Veg
http://www.newveg.av.org

Vegetarian Pages
http://www.veg.org/veg/

Veggies Unite!
http://www.vegweb.com

VegSource
http://www.vegsource.com

Index

A

Aaron, Hank, 15
animal products and health, 21–23
    and cancer, 21
    and cholesterol, 21
    and diabetes, 21
    and heart disease, 21
    and nutrition, 25

B

Basinger, Kim, 15
Bernard Shaw, George, 14

C

calcium, 41

D

Da Vinci, Leonardo, 13
dairy product alternatives, 32–34
    and nut milk, 33
    and rice milk, 33, 41
    and soy cheese, 33–34, 56
    and soy milk, 33
dairy products, 8, 11, 12, 32, 41
diet, 6, 36, 40, 41, 43, 49

E

Edison, Thomas, 14
Einstein, Albert, 14
environmental problems, 20–21
ethics, 18
    and antibiotics, 19
    and disease, 19
    and factory farms, 19, 20
    and free-range, 20
    and hormones, 19
    and methods of slaughter, 19–20
    and overcrowding, 19

ethnic foods, 34–38
    Asian, 34–36
    Italian, 36
    Mexican, 36–37
    Middle Eastern, 36

G

gelatin, 12–13, 27
Gilbert, Sara, 15
grains, 31–32

H

health food, 14, 31
Hoffman, Dustin, 15

I

iron, 41–42
    and menstruation, 42

J

Jackson, Michael, 15
Johnson, Kathy, 15

L

lacto vegetarians, 12
lard, 12
leather, 11, 20, 27

M

Martin, Steve, 15
McCartney, Paul, 15
meat substitutes, 17, 31
Merchant, Natalie, 15

N

Navratilova, Martina, 14
nutrients, 7, 22, 25, 27, 30,
    40–43

O
organic food, 20
ovo-lacto vegetarians, 11–12, 43

P
Plato, 13
protein, 25, 30, 33, 40–41
Pythagoras, 13

R
recipes, 52–56
    hummus, 52–54
    tofu-vegetable stir-fry, 55–56
    vanilla fruit smoothie, 56
    vegetable soup, 54–55
restaurant, 6, 28, 34, 37, 52

S
Shakespeare, William, 14
Socrates, 13
soy, 8, 22, 30–31, 34, 40, 41

T
tempeh, 7, 31, 52
tofu (bean curd), 7, 30–31, 34, 38, 41

V
vegan, 11, 22, 25, 27, 32, 34, 39, 41
vegetarianism and health benefits,
        43–45
    and cancer, 43
    and heart disease, 44
    and diabetes, 44
vitamin B_{12}, 42–43
    and anemia, 42
    and fatigue, 42
    and nerve damage, 42
vitamins, 7, 12, 25, 42–43

W
Wollstonecraft Shelley, Mary, 14
wool, 11, 20

About the Author

Kim Serafin is a writer and an actress from New York City currently living in Los Angeles. She has a background in politics, having served as a deputy press secretary to Rudolph Giuliani, mayor of New York City, and to Richard Riordan, mayor of Los Angeles. She holds a B.A. from New York University's Gallatin School with a concentration in journalism and politics.

Photo Credits

Cover Photo by Simca Israelian. Pp. 15, 18 © Everett Collection; pp. 21, 23 © UNIPHOTO Stock Agency; pp. 30, 40 © Stock Food America/Eising; p. 33 © Stock Food America/Usbeck; p. 35 © Stock Food America/Mastri; p. 37 © Stock Food America/Arras; p. 50 © Keith Aden; p. 53 © Stock Food America/DeSantos. All other photos by Simca Israelian.